hanson

It's all here—awesome photos, tons of trivia, and quizzes to test your Hanson IQ!

★ What prop does Zac use for effect during live performances of "Man from Milwaukee"?

★ How old was Tay when *Middle of Nowhere* was released?

★ What pet animal does Ike sometimes take with him on the road?

★ What are the best places on-line to learn about *your* favorite bro?

Find all these answers and more in . . .

Hanson: The Ultimate Trivia Book

Look for other biographies from Archway Paperbacks

hanson
THE ULTIMATE TRIVIA BOOK!

matt netter

AN ARCHWAY PAPERBACK
Published by POCKET BOOKS
New York London Toronto Sydney Tokyo Singapore

AN ARCHWAY PAPERBACK *Original*

An Archway Paperback published by
POCKET BOOKS, a division of Simon & Schuster Inc.
1230 Avenue of the Americas, New York, NY 10020

Copyright © 1998 by Matt Netter

ISBN: 0-671-02488-4

First Archway Paperback printing March 1998

10 9 8 7 6 5 4 3 2 1

AN ARCHWAY PAPERBACK and colophon are
registered trademarks of Simon & Schuster Inc.

Cover photo © David Lachapelle/Outline

Printed in the U.S.A.

IL 4+

This book is dedicated to bright young minds—without them the world would be a passionless place. You are all perfect in your own way . . . especially Melissa N.

CONTENTS

INTRODUCTION

With millions of fans all over the world, Hanson mania has reached epidemic proportions. In 1997 many of these fans got hooked on Hanson's feel-good pop music, while others just got stuck on one of the three brotherly babes. However, a portion of Hanson supporters know every song by heart and must get their hands on every photo, article, and piece of information they can find on the band. Put simply, they are Hanson fanatics.

Are you a Hanson fanatic? Answer the following questions: Do you have so many pictures and posters of Isaac, Taylor, and Zachary hanging in your bedroom that you can barely tell what color the walls are painted? Do you regularly surf the Net and buy teen magazines to find the latest on Hanson? Do you send creative fan letters and drawings to the group? Do you set the VCR every time they appear on TV? Did your Christmas stocking contain the Hanson tour video, *Tulsa, Tokyo and the Middle of Nowhere* and their holiday CD, *Snowed In?* If you answered yes to most or all of these questions, then you are indeed cuckoo for Cocoa Puffs over Hanson!

Millions of fan letters are sent to Hanson HITZ, the group's fan club, and to Mercury, their record company, every month. Many of them are written by fanatics who proclaim that *they* are Hanson's number one fan. So many such letters are sent to *Teen Beat* magazine that their Mail Call section has become a forum for a war among fans. A typical letter reads: "How could Jennifer from Okonomowac, Wisconsin, think *she's* Hanson's number one when she doesn't even have *Boomerang?* Besides, I have way more pinups than she does!"

While the brothers appreciate all of their fans equally, the fierce competition among their loyal followers continues. Friends and classmates constantly turn to magazines, Websites, radio stations, MTV, and one another to see who knows the most about Ike, Tay, and Zac. So it seems that the true measure of your devotion is the extent of your Hanson knowledge. This book provides over 200 trivia questions to test your Hanson know-how, plus little-known facts and a scoring section to see how you measure up against other fans. There's also a bonus Website chapter to help you find out even more about Hanson. Have fun!

hanson
THE ULTIMATE TRIVIA BOOK!

1

BAND BASICS

Ike, Tay, and Zac were getting out of a van for an interview when they heard "MMMBop" on the radio for the first time. They hopped back in the van and cranked up the volume!

So you call yourself a Hanson fan, huh? If you are, you should know all about the childhood of Isaac, Taylor, and Zachary as well as all the details behind how they became a band. The Hanson brothers had a unique upbringing that involved a big family, a nontraditional education, and lots of travel. Their road to fame was filled with hard work, a little luck, and a lot of interesting stories. Take this 25-question quiz to see how well you know the story behind Hanson:

1. What city do the Hanson brothers call home?

2. How many Hanson siblings are there?

3. What are their mom's and dad's names?

4. When the Hanson brothers are home, where do they practice?

5. What fun things are in the Hanson backyard at home?

6. What toys do the boys collect?

7. True or false: The Hanson boys all go to private school.

8. Dad played guitar and sang in a church choir when he was younger, but he never seriously pursued a career in music. How does he earn a living?

9. The Hansons moved several times because of Dad's international career. In what three countries, beside the United States, have they lived?

10. What music was the inspiration for Hanson's songwriting?

11. Where did Ike, Tay, and Zac present their first show, an unrehearsed *a cappella* performance of doo-wop songs in front of a small crowd?

12. At which Tulsa club did the boys have to play outside in the parking lot?

13. At what fair did Hanson first perform on the community stage?

14. Hanson first met their manager at the South

by Southwest Music Conference. Where was that conference held?

15. What is the band manager's name?

16. What Mercury Records executive signed them to their contract?

17. Where did the Hanson family live temporarily during the recording of *Middle of Nowhere?*

18. How old were Ike, Tay, and Zac when *Middle of Nowhere* was released?

19. To Zac, Tay, and Ike, what are the three most important things in life?

20. What is the one true rock group that Hanson has always admired?

21. What does "HITZ" in Hanson's fan club address stand for?

22. True or false: All three brothers took piano lessons as young children.

23. True or false: At one point they all took dance lessons.

24. What item did their dad advise the Hansons always to take with them when they're on the road?

25. What date did Oklahoma's governor proclaim Hanson Day?

Answers to Band Basics Quiz

Early on, when they were called the Hanson Brothers, the boys sported pageboy haircuts and wore matching black leather jackets onstage.

1. Ike, Tay, and Zac were born in Tulsa, Oklahoma, where their family and most of their relatives still live.

2. Seven. Isaac, Taylor, Zachary, little sisters Jessica and Avery, little brother Mackenzie, and a newborn baby!

3. Diana and Walker.

4. In the garage.

5. A soccer goal, a half pipe for skateboarding and in-line skating, and a treehouse that family members built.

6. Lego blocks.

7. False. They are home-schooled by Mom, Diana, and by other tutors.

8. He's an executive at a Tulsa area oil company.

9. Venezuela, Ecuador, and Trinidad.

10. The Time/Life series tapes that they took with them to the Caribbean and South America. The tapes featured classics of the 1950s and 1960s by great musicians like Chuck Berry and Aretha Franklin.

11. At a family Christmas party at Walker's company.

12. The Blue Rose Café.

13. Tulsa's Mayfest.

14. In Austin, Texas.

15. Christopher Sabec.

16. Steve Greenberg.

17. Los Angeles, California.

18. Sixteen, fourteen, and eleven.

19. Family, religion, and music.

20. Aerosmith.

21. Hanson, Isaac, Taylor, Zachary.

22. True.

23. True.

24. A journal in which to record their experiences.

25. May 6.

2

ZAC'S POP QUIZ

Zachary's never met a dessert he didn't like. He especially goes for Twinkies, Ding Dongs, chocolate ice cream, and green Jell-O.

Twelve-year-old Zachary is as cute as a kitten and as energetic as one, too! He's a talented singer and songwriter, and he's the youngest drummer in rock and roll. Zac loves to have fun, and he seeks attention at every turn. He achieves both by doing whatever it takes to get a crowd fired up. These 25 questions will test your knowledge of Hanson's little spitfire:

1. True or false: Zachary is really his middle name.

2. What grade is Zac in?

3. When is his birthday?

4. What is his zodiac sign?

5. What nickname have Ike and Tay given him?

6. What clothing item does Zac take the most pride in?

7. After stopping home and seeing his family, where is the first place Zac likes to go to in Tulsa?

8. How old was Zac when he and his brothers first got serious about music?

9. True or false: Zac doesn't watch much TV.

10. On what two songs on *Middle of Nowhere* does Zac sing lead?

11. Where was Hanson when Zac pretended a tennis racket was a guitar?

12. What items has Zac collected from hotels in the cities where Hanson has been?

13. When Hanson appeared on *Fox After Breakfast*, what guest did Zac taunt?

14. What is Zac's favorite color?

15. What talk show was Zac most excited about appearing on?

16. Zac sings lead on two songs and part of another on the holiday album, *Snowed In*. Name them.

17. Zac's first set of drums came from a friend's attic. What embarrassment did the drum set

cause the band at one of their first live shows?

18. During a recording session at the Dust Brothers' house, Zac played drums on one song while soaking wet. How did this happen?

19. What does Zac call excited Hanson fans?

20. True or false: Zac's favorite restaurant is Burger King?

21. What is that small black ball that Zac holds and shakes during *a cappella* renditions of songs?

22. What prop does Zac use for effect during live performances of "Man from Milwaukee"?

23. When "MMMBop" reached the number one spot on the *Billboard* singles chart, Zac was eleven years and six months old. Who was the only musician to reach that coveted spot at an even younger age?

24. During what concert did Zac bring a shy girl from the crowd onstage?

25. Zachary jokes that a younger Hanson sibling might someday take over behind the drum set. Which sibling is he referring to?

Answers to Zac's Pop Quiz

While other kids his age look forward to Christmas all year, Zac's favorite holiday is Halloween. He may be a big star, but Zac still likes to dress up in costume and even go trick-or-treating!

1. False. Zachary is the only member of Hanson to go by his real first name. His middle name is Walker, after his dad.

2. Zac is home-schooled, but he is the equivalent of a sixth grader.

3. October 22, 1985.

4. Libra.

5. "Animal," after the zany Muppets character who also plays the drums.

6. His Doc Marten shoes.

7. LaserQuest.

8. He was only six years old.

9. True. Aside from not having much free time

for TV, Zac prefers playing outdoors to being a couch potato.

10. "Man from Milwaukee" and "Lucy."

11. They were performing a benefit concert in Flushing, New York, for the opening of Arthur Ashe Stadium.

12. Miniature shampoo bottles.

13. Actress Kathy Griffin of *Suddenly Susan*.

14. Blue, although rumor has it his toothbrush is lime green.

15. *The Late Show with David Letterman*.

16. Zac sings lead on "Rockin' Around the Christmas Tree" and "What Christmas Means to Me." He also gets to showcase his pipes in parts of "Silent Night Medley."

17. The bass drum came loose and started rolling across the stage. Zac and his brothers had to chase it down!

18. He jumped into the Dust Brothers' pool with all his clothes on.

19. The Scream Squad.

20. False. Zac likes to eat at a Tulsa restaurant called Rex's Boneless Chicken.

21. A mini-maraca.

22. A megaphone.

23. Michael Jackson was eleven years and five months old when the Jackson 5 hit number one with "I Want You Back."

24. It was at a Tulsa area show in a school gymnasium before Hanson was even signed to a recording contract.

25. His three-year-old brother Mackenzie.

3

TAYLOR TEST

Taylor's favorite performers are Counting Crows, Spin Doctors, Billy Joel, and Natalie Merchant, but he also has a soft spot for some oldies but goodies. Chuck Berry, Little Richard, Otis Redding, Aretha Franklin, the Beatles, and the Jackson 5 all have a place on Tay's CD shelf.

Let's face it, as beautiful as his voice is and as well as he plays keyboard, many fans live for Taylor for the simple fact that he is gorgeous. In fact, if Tay weren't a famous and successful musician, you'd probably still like him just because you can't stop staring into his beautiful baby blues. By now you've probably done your best to dig up every speck of dirt about Tay. Take this quiz to see if you know him as well as you think:

1. What is Taylor's middle name?

2. When was he born?

3. What is his zodiac sign?

4. How old was Tay when he began taking piano lessons?

5. What is Taylor's favorite sport?

6. Which of the following instruments does Tay play:
   a) tambourine b) bongos and conga
   c) keyboard d) all of the above

7. What is Tay's favorite color?

8. True or false: Taylor is accident-prone.

9. What is Tay's favorite saying?

10. True or false: Tay is left-handed.

11. True or false: Tay's shoe size is 13.

12. Which of the three actresses on *Friends*—Courtney Cox, Jennifer Aniston, or Lisa Kudrow—has Tay admitted to having a crush on?

13. True or false: Taylor has a sweet tooth.

14. What drink does he usually take with him everywhere?

15. True or false: Tay's hair is now longer than it's ever been.

16. What is Tay's favorite word?

17. Where did Tay get his first keyboard?

18. What articles of jewelry does Taylor like to wear?

19. Does Taylor consider himself Hanson's lead singer?

20. Which of the following is *not* one of Tay's hobbies:
a) drawing b) in-line skating c) stamp collecting d) playing video games

21. What handheld instrument does Taylor sometimes play during unplugged songs?

22. Why does Taylor warn people not to go near his bedroom closet?

23. What kind of movies does Taylor like?

24. What album was Tay speaking of when he said, "Listen to every song because there is a huge variety. One makes you want to dance, one makes you feel good, one is really intense, and another is really mellow."

25. True or false: Taylor describes himself as "stupid-goofy."

ANSWERS TO TAYLOR TEST

Like any typical teen, Taylor breaks for fast food, but when it comes time for a home-cooked meal, he opts for fish and Mom's homemade brownies.

1. Taylor *is* his middle name. His first name is Jordan, but he has always been called Taylor.

2. March 14, 1983.

3. Pisces.

4. Eight years old.

5. Soccer.

6. d.

7. Red.

8. True. Tay has two scars on his face from running into a glass door and one on his leg from playing soccer. He also once broke his arm in a bicycle accident.

9. "Everything changes."

10. False. He's ambidextrous.

11. True.

12. Jennifer Aniston.

13. True. Tay especially loves jelly beans and strawberry ice cream.

14. Bottled water.

15. False. Tay's hair was once more than six inches longer than it is now. He maintains that tightly braided rat tail as a reminder.

16. "Weird."

17. At a pawnshop in Tulsa.

18. Chokers.

19. No. Although he sings lead on ten of the thirteen songs on *Middle of Nowhere* Tay says, "A lot of groups have one singer, but the thing that makes us Hanson is that there's three guys who can all sing."

20. c.

21. Tambourine.

22. It's filled with dirty socks.

23. Action movies and comedies.

24. *Middle of Nowhere.*

25. False. Zac is the one who describes himself as "stupid-goofy." Tay considers himself "the quiet one."

4

ISAAC EXAM

To ease the tension before a big show, Ike will sometimes crack his brothers up with dead-on impersonations of cartoon characters like Beavis and Butt-head and Scooby Doo.

Hanson's oldest bro is a brilliant singer, songwriter, and guitarist, and he's one of the coolest cats in all of pop music. With his beautiful locks and confident grin, it's hard to believe that's not a longtime rock star behind those sunglasses. It took just one year for Ike to garner the respect of other musicians and the adoration of fans around the world. How much do you like Ike? To find out, see how many of these questions you can answer:

1. How old was Isaac when he wrote his first complete song?

2. What was its title?

3. Which song on *Middle of Nowhere* does Isaac sing lead on?

4. When is Isaac's birthday?

5. What is his horoscope sign?

6. He's gone by his middle name, Isaac, since birth. What's his first name?

7. Aside from making silly home videos, what did Isaac use his camcorder for?

8. True or false: Isaac's favorite sports are football and baseball.

9. What's Ike's favorite color?

10. Because Isaac is tall and loves the movie *Star Wars*, Taylor has given him a certain nickname. What is it?

11. True or false: Ike wears chokers, like his brother Tay.

12. Which of the following places is Ike most likely to stop at for a bite:
a) McDonald's b) Wendy's c) Domino's Pizza d) Burger King

13. True or false: Isaac is the only Hanson brother who has a driver's license.

14. True or false: Isaac's braces are metal.

15. If Tay is "the quiet one" and Zac is "the wacky one," how have people labeled Ike?

16. What pet animal does Ike sometimes take with him on the road?

17. True or false: Isaac's first guitar was a Christmas present from his parents.

18. Is Ike left- or right-handed?

19. Ike once wrote a special song called "I'll Show You Mars." What special person did he write it for?

20. In the *Tulsa, Tokyo and the Middle of Nowhere* video, Isaac got a chance to meet his celebrity crush. Who is it?

21. In which of the following ways does Ike wear his hair:
    a) ponytail b) braids c) dreadlocks
    d) all of the above

22. What grade is Isaac in?

23. Who was Isaac's inspiration to become a guitar player?

24. What item does Isaac take with him on the road to remind him of home?

25. Which songs on *Snowed In* does Isaac sing lead on?

Answers to Isaac Exam

Since he was too young to know about relationships and real life problems, Isaac wrote his first songs about ants and frogs!

1. Eight years old.

2. "Rain Falling Down."

3. "A Minute Without You."

4. November 17, 1980.

5. Scorpio.

6. Clarke.

7. Some of the scenes in *Tulsa, Tokyo and the Middle of Nowhere.*

8. False. Ike's into in-line skating and street hockey.

9. Green.

10. Chewbacca.

11. False. The only jewelry Ike sports is a silver

ring, which he wears on the middle finger of his left hand, and a wristwatch.

12. c.

13. True. Tay will get his license in 1999.

14. False. They are clear plastic.

15. "The serious one."

16. His turtle.

17. False. He bought a used guitar at a pawnshop.

18. Right-handed.

19. His little brother Mackenzie.

20. Supermodel Cindy Crawford.

21. a.

22. Ike is home-schooled, but he's the equivalent of a high school junior.

23. His dad, Walker, played guitar for years.

24. A snow globe of Tulsa that his friends from home gave him.

25. "Little Saint Nick," "At Christmas," "Run Rudolph Run," and part of "Silent Night Medley."

5

WHO SAID THAT?

Zac once said, "I'm not gonna get married in the next five or six years." It's a good thing he feels that way because it's illegal to get married in most states before you're eighteen.

If you've got a four-foot stack of magazines with Hanson articles in them, then maybe you can ace this test. This section contains 25 Hanson quotes from various interviews and press conferences from around the world. Read each quote and see if you can determine whether Isaac, Taylor, or Zachary said it:

1. "You can't expect success. You can only hope for it."

2. "There's three brothers that enjoy hanging out with each other who love what they're doing. That's just who we are. We're just normal guys having fun with it."

3. "We're best friends, only bester."

4. "Our parents are completely behind us and they always have been. They've always said, 'You can stop if you want to and we'll be totally behind you.' I think their best advice is 'You have to love it.'"

5. "It would be important for someone to understand how much our music means to us. Our music comes first right now and, hopefully, forever."

6. "Music can't be about fame and money or any of that stuff. You have to really love it."

7. "We know that the kind of success we're having may not last forever. Success can go as fast as it comes. We all realize that. Anyone who doesn't realize that is in trouble, because they could lose touch with reality."

8. "Not everyone is going to like our music. People say, 'Oh, they're just kids. They don't really play.' We do play and we write our own music, too. We believe that our music speaks for itself."

9. "Maybe people don't hate their parents so much these days."

10. "Everybody has their opinion, that's part of life. It's fine, you know?"

11. "When we first started playing instruments,

we weren't doing very much—just simple stuff. Bang, bang, bang!"

12. "We were writing songs about girls when we still thought girls had cooties."

13. "We get our ideas for the songs from what happens to us in our lives on a daily basis. If you're creative, anything may inspire you, from hanging out with friends to just staring out your window at passing scenes."

14. "Actually my voice is pretty much done changing. But it was pretty bad when we were making the album."

15. "Omigosh, Sears is having a sale!"

16. "The nice thing about England is they actually speak English."

17. "Sometimes it feels like the girls aren't screaming at us. They're screaming at some band called Hanson they saw on TV."

18. "We're allowed to date, but the girlfriend thing probably wouldn't be a good idea. A girl would probably not want to deal with me."

19. "I'm still looking for a girlfriend. I just don't think I've met the right one yet. Maybe someday."

20. "Girls are just icing on the cake, or music is like a hot dog and girls are the condiments.

Life is a Twinkie and girls are the sticky white stuff inside."

21. "If somebody's obsessed with you, it would be kind of hard to go out with her. You'd take her hand and she'll scream! But if she was nice enough, yeah, I'd date a fan."

22. "Let's see, I missed out on getting dumped by about ten million girls, getting beat up by bullies, and peer pressure."

23. "I used to be the goofiest, and then Zac just kind of took over."

24. "I think it's probably actually that I'm so shy that I just act wacky to make up for it."

25. "How much better of a job could you possibly have than to be in a band for the rest of your whole life?"

Answers to Who Said That?

> "We want to say right now that we're not going to put out Hanson dolls," Tay confirmed. "We're not going to put out totally sell-out stuff."

1. Zac

2. Taylor

3. Zac

4. Taylor

5. Isaac

6. Taylor

7. Isaac

8. Taylor

9. Zac (on the fading-out of alternative rock)

10. Taylor (on Hanson haters)

11. Zac

12. Zac

13. Isaac

14. Taylor

15. Isaac (after seeing how many fans showed up for their Paramus Mall concert)

16. Isaac

17. Taylor

18. Isaac

19. Zac

20. Zac

21. Taylor

22. Isaac (when asked if he regretted not having gone to public school)

23. Isaac

24. Zac

25. Taylor

6

DISCOGRAPHY

Early on in their musical careers, before they began playing instruments, the Hanson brothers were more often compared to New Edition than to the Jackson 5.

How many times have you listened to your Hanson CDs? A hundred times? A thousand or more? Do you know which brother sings lead on each song? How about where each album was recorded and where each video was filmed? Do you know who cowrote some of the songs with Hanson? Are you up on your order of events? If you can answer all 50 of these questions correctly, you're more than a fan—you're a fanatic!

1. What are the titles of Hanson's two earlier independent albums?

2. Hanson's sound on their first independent CD was very different from *Middle of Nowhere*. What kind of music were they making back then?

3. How many of the songs on their first independent CD were original Hanson compositions?

4. The first independent CD contained a cover of a Jackson 5 song. What is the title of that song?

5. How many tracks are on their second independent CD?

6. What is special about the inside of the second independent CD's cover?

7. How many songs from the second of these two albums appeared on *Middle of Nowhere*?

8. Where was *Middle of Nowhere* recorded?

9. Who produced *Middle of Nowhere*?

10. What was the release date of *Middle of Nowhere*?

11. How many songs are on *Middle of Nowhere*?

12. When was "MMMBop" first played on the radio?

13. At what number did "MMMBop" debut on the *Billboard* singles chart when it was first released as a single?

14. Who sings lead on "MMMBop"?

15. Who sings lead on "Where's the Love"?

16. Who helped Hanson write "Weird"?

17. Where did the idea for "Lucy" come from?

18. What is the song "Yearbook" about?

19. What three songs on *Middle of Nowhere* did musician-turned-songwriter Mark Hudson cowrite with Hanson?

20. Who is the song "With You in Your Dreams" written about?

21. Who helped Hanson write "Yearbook"?

22. The famous songwriting duo, Barry Mann and Cynthia Weil, wrote such romantic hits as "You've Lost That Lovin' Feeling." What song did they cowrite on *Middle of Nowhere*?

23. What Grammy Award–winning album did the Dust Brothers produce before lending a hand with *Middle of Nowhere*?

24. Who cowrote "Madeline" with Hanson?

25. What does "MMMBop" mean?

26. What is "MMMBop" about?

27. Complete the following lyric from "Look at You": "Out of the corner of my eye she said . . ."

28. Which Hanson brother is largely responsible for "Man from Milwaukee?"

29. What song is the following lyric from: "You are my ten thousand roses and I let you go"?

30. What is "Madeline" about?

31. What is Hanson's favorite song on *Middle of Nowhere?*

32. In what city did Hanson film the video for "Where's the Love?"

33. Where was the "MMMBop" video filmed?

34. Who directed these two videos?

35. True or false: The Hanson brothers performed all their own stunts in the "MMMBop" video.

36. What prop in the video was from the movie *Speed 2?*

37. Where was the video for "I Will Come to You" filmed?

38. The "I Will Come to You" video is special for two reasons. What are they?

39. To whom did Hanson dedicate their Christmas album, *Snowed In?*

40. What date was the Christmas album released?

41. Who coproduced *Snowed In* with Hanson?

42. How many songs on *Snowed In* are original Hanson compositions?

43. Where was *Snowed In* recorded?

44. How many songs are on *Snowed In?*

45. Who sings lead on "At Christmas"?

46. What three Christmas songs does the "Silent Night Medley" comprise?

47. Who sings lead on "Christmas Time"?

48. Who sings lead on "Everybody Knows the Claus"?

49. True or false: Taylor sings lead on "Merry Christmas, Baby."

50. What are Zac, Ike, and Tay wrapped up in on the cover of *Snowed In?*

Answers to Discography Quiz

Before Hanson was signed to a record deal, the boys had already written over two hundred songs!

1. *Boomerang* and *MMMBop*.

2. R&B, mostly *a cappella*.

3. Five. The other four songs on *Boomerang* were covers.

4. "The Love You Save."

5. Fifteen, including two versions of "MMMBop."

6. It includes drawings made by Ike, Tay, and Zac.

7. Three: "Thinking of You," "With You in Your Dreams," and "MMMBop."

8. Los Angeles.

9. Stephen Lironi and the Dust Brothers.

10. May 6, 1997.

11. Twelve, plus the CD bonus track "Man from Milwaukee."

12. March 24, 1997.

13. Number 16.

14. Taylor.

15. Taylor.

16. Desmond Child.

17. A *Peanuts* cartoon strip lithograph that hangs on the wall in songwriter Mark Hudson's office.

18. A missing classmate.

19. "Where's the Love," "Lucy," and "A Minute Without You."

20. The Hansons' late grandmother.

21. Ellen Shipley.

22. "I Will Come to You."

23. Beck's *Odelay*.

24. Cliff Magness.

25. It's a short moment in time.

26. How easy it is to fall out of touch with the people in your life.

27. "Why don't you come and give it a try?"

28. Zac. The song is loosely based on an experience he had while waiting at a bus stop in Albuquerque, New Mexico.

29. "Madeline"

30. An on-again, off-again relationship.

31. They don't have a favorite. They like them all.

32. London.

33. Los Angeles.

34. Tamra Davis.

35. True. In fact, as Zac has pointed out, "The skating wipeouts were real. Definitely real."

36. The Humvee that Taylor drives is the same car that Sandra Bullock drove in the movie.

37. The Beacon Theater in New York City.

38. (1) Fans in the audience got to be in the video, and (2) it was part of a performance that was featured in *Tulsa, Tokyo and the Middle of Nowhere*.

39. Their fans.

40. November 18, 1997.

41. Mark Hudson.

42. Three: "At Christmas," "Christmas Time," and "Everybody Knows the Claus."

43. England.

44. Eleven.

45. Isaac.

46. "O Holy Night," "Silent Night," and "O Come All Ye Faithful."

47. Taylor.

48. Taylor.

49. True, although Taylor does alter his voice slightly. He exaggerates the raspiness of his voice to complement the funky mood of the song.

50. Christmas lights.

7

APPEARANCE IS EVERYTHING

Things got so out of hand at Hanson's mall concert in Melbourne, Australia, that the boys needed a police escort just to get out of the mall!

You've been there since the beginning. From the first time "MMMBop" aired on the radio to where the band is appearing this week, you've been hot on the Hanson trail from day one. You've been attending or reading about all of their performances and watching all of their TV appearances. You even stayed up late to watch them on *Saturday Night Live!* If this sounds like you, then maybe you'll do okay on these 50 stumpers. Good luck. You'll need it.

1. Following the release of their debut CD, in what city did Hanson embark on a two-week media blitz?

2. Which of the following magazine covers has Hanson appeared on:

a) *Seventeen* b) *Spin* c) *Rolling Stone* d) all of the above

3. The day after *Middle of Nowhere* was released, Hanson staged a mini-concert at a mall in Paramus, New Jersey. Mall security expected a few hundred people to show up. How many actually came?

4. Some live footage for *Tulsa, Tokyo and the Middle of Nowhere* was filmed during a special performance. Where did this event occur?

5. Where were the Hanson brothers when they were unable to receive a special award from the governor of Oklahoma?

6. What famous mall's parking lot did Hanson fill for a Jam Against Hunger benefit concert?

7. What talk show host referred to Hanson as "cutie patooties"?

8. What comedic actor pretended to be the fourth member of Hanson during the 1997 MTV Movie Awards broadcast?

9. Why did Zac dress up in a bright yellow motorcycle outfit for Hanson's B-96 FM promotional concert in Chicago?

10. On *Saturday Night Live* Hanson did more than just play a few tunes. They also appeared in a comedy skit. What *SNL* cast

member and what TV actress starred in it with them?

11. What was the *SNL* skit about?

12. For the B-96 FM promotional concert, Hanson and two other artists sold out Chicago's Rosemont Horizon arena. Who were the other two? Hint: one was a group and the other was a solo artist.

13. Where did Hanson perform with many other bands as part of a two-day charity festival?

14. What was the name of the huge Christmas concert at New York's Madison Square Garden where Hanson and other bands performed?

15. True or false: During Hanson's radio promotional tour in the fall of 1997, the group performed as many as three shows each day.

16. Which of the following bands did *not* join Hanson for the Y-100 Wing-Ding benefit concert in south Florida:
a) Bush b) Ziggy Marley and the Melody Makers c) 98° d) Duncan Sheik

17. At what concert did Hanson steal the spotlight from the world's best tennis players?

18. Although it was canceled due to stormy skies, a top-ranked female tennis player was

supposed to play a fun match against Hanson. Who was it?

19. What Nickelodeon stars were on hand that day to sign autographs and hand out free burgers?

20. Who was the emcee of the event?

21. True or false: Hanson played only two songs that day, "MMMBop" and "Where's the Love."

22. Which Hanson brother did photographers complain they couldn't get photos of at Arthur Ashe Stadium?

23. A homemade Hanson short film was shown in the *Tulsa, Tokyo and the Middle of Nowhere* video. What was the subject of that film?

24. When did Zac drive a crowd crazy by pretending to jump over a railing?

25. Which of the following morning shows has Hanson appeared on:
a) *Good Morning America* b) *Live with Regis & Kathie Lee* c) *Fox After Breakfast* d) all of the above

26. Which late night talk show has the band *never* appeared on:
a) *The Late Show with David Letterman*

b) The Tonight Show with Jay Leno
c) Late Night with Conan O'Brien

27. What legendary host introduced Hanson on the ABC-TV *American Bandstand* special?

28. What was the name of that TV special?

29. What songs from *Middle of Nowhere* did Hanson play during that special?

30. Only one song was *not* performed unplugged. What was it?

31. What talk show host asked each of Hanson's backup musicians, "Are you a Hanson?"

32. What unforgettable thing did the band do after their *Fox After Breakfast* interview?

33. On what cable show did Ike, Tay, and Zac mention that they weren't big fans of Barney?

34. Hanson couldn't make it to the MTV Video Music Awards at New York City's Radio City Music Hall in September, so instead they prerecorded an interview with MTV. Where did it take place?

35. When did Hanson meet actor Jack Nicholson?

36. "Cooking with Hanson" was part of a special on what network?

37. Which of the following did Hanson do at the MTV Europe Music Awards?
a) present awards b) receive awards
c) perform d) all of the above

38. What awards did they receive?

39. After meeting a famous group for the first time, Zac remarked, "They're all very short." What group was he referring to?

40. In what city did a radio reporter compare Zac to Michael Jackson and then jokingly ask him if he intended to have cosmetic surgery?

41. In what city did the Hanson boys go on a Doc Martens shoe-shopping spree?

42. While in Europe, Hanson visited all of the following countries except one. Which one did they *not* visit?
a) Italy b) Spain c) Germany d) France

43. Where did the photography and interview for Hanson's *Entertainment Weekly* cover story take place?

44. In what two Australian cities did Hanson perform?

45. In which Australian city did some lucky fans go for a boat ride with Hanson?

46. In what city were fans waiting for Hanson at the airport gate when they got off the plane?

47. How many people showed up for the concert in this city?

48. In what foreign city did Hanson fans have to be escorted in groups past the band by officials to avoid total mayhem?

49. In what city did an overwhelming mob of fans become so frenzied that Hanson had to end their Hard Rock Cafe performance in midsong?

50. How many continents has Hanson toured in?

ANSWERS TO APPEARANCE IS EVERYTHING QUIZ

At the Beacon Theater concert in New York, fans chanted "Hanson! Hanson! Hanson!" until Ike, Tay, and Zac ran onstage shooting Silly String into the crowd!

1. New York City.

2. a.

3. Six thousand.

4. At the Beacon Theater in New York City.

5. They were in New York, taping their segment for *The Late Show with David Letterman*.

6. The Mall of America in Bloomington, Minnesota.

7. Rosie O'Donnell.

8. *Just Shoot Me* star David Spade.

9. It was Halloween.

10. *Saturday Night Live* cast member Will Ferrel and *Mad About You* star Helen Hunt.

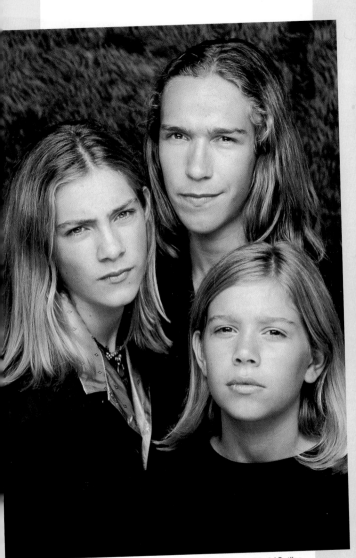

Frank W. Ockenfels 3 / Outline

Todd Kaplan / Star File

Frank W.Ockenfels 3 / Outline

11. Ferrel and Hunt played terrorists who held Zac, Tay, and Ike hostage in an elevator and made them listen to "MMMBop" over and over until it drove them crazy.

12. Backstreet Boys and Robyn.

13. South Florida, for the annual Y-100 Wing-Ding event.

14. The Z-100 Jingle Ball.

15. True. In fact, at one point Hanson performed eight radio shows in three days. From November 19 to November 21 they were in Detroit, Cleveland, Washington, D.C., Baltimore, Philadelphia, Pittsburgh, Columbus, and Atlanta! Talk about frequent fliers!

16. a.

17. At the USTA Arthur Ashe Kids' Day in August 1997.

18. Martina Hingis.

19. Kel Mitchell and Kenan Thompson of *All That, Kenan & Kel,* and *Good Burger* fame.

20. Bill Cosby.

21. False. In between the tennis matches Hanson did indeed play those two songs, but after the matches were over, Hanson came on

again to jam some more for the delighted crowd!

22. Zachary. It was hard to see him behind the drum set the way the stage was set up.

23. Redwood trees.

24. In Los Angeles, during Hanson's performance outside Sam Goody at Universal City Walk.

25. d.

26. c.

27. Dick Clark.

28. *Meet Hanson.*

29. "MMMBop," "Man from Milwaukee," "I Will Come to You," and "Madeline."

30. "MMMBop."

31. David Letterman.

32. They played a live set outside the building that caused a traffic jam on New York's Fifth Avenue.

33. MTV's *Jenny McCarthy Show.*

34. New York City's Central Park.

35. When they were musical guests on *Saturday Night Live,* Jack Nicholson showed up to

surprise Helen Hunt, his costar in *As Good As It Gets.*

36. It was on Nickelodeon, when Hanson hosted a Saturday evening of SNICK programming.

37. d.

38. Best Breakthrough Act and Best Song, for "MMMBop."

39. The Spice Girls.

40. Paris.

41. London.

42. b.

43. London.

44. Melbourne and Sydney.

45. Sydney. Some radio contest winners got to join Hanson on a ferry across Sydney Harbor.

46. Melbourne, Australia.

47. Over 20,000! Many camped out from the night before to ensure a good view of the band.

48. Tokyo.

49. Djakarta, Indonesia.

50. Four: North America, Europe, Asia, and Australia. South America and Africa may not be far off, but don't count on Ike, Tay, and Zac performing on mountains of ice in Antarctica!

8

NEW AND UPCOMING

Isaac, Taylor, and Zachary have often been compared to the Jackson 5 because they're a family act that makes sweet harmony. But one thing the groups will never have in common is a Saturday morning cartoon series. Hanson has disavowed rumors of such a project.

With such a groundbreaking year behind them, countless opportunities lie ahead for Hanson. From world tours to Hollywood movies, the blond trio's options are endless. To stay on top of the very latest Hanson news you've got to act like a reporter and remain on the beat at all times. If you've been reading all the magazine articles, listening to all the MTV and radio reports, and continually checking up on the Websites, then just maybe you know what the future holds for Hanson. Test your reporter skills with this test:

1. When Hanson signed their record deal with Mercury, how many albums did they agree to make?

2. True or false: Hanson is going to make a *My Three Sons*-type movie.

3. Will they make a movie about their lives?

4. Who is the movie's producer?

5. Who has been signed on to write the screenplay?

6. What future project did Hanson recently discuss on *Entertainment Tonight?*

7. If Hanson ever had a TV show, would it be a drama or comedy?

8. Can we look forward to the sale of Hanson dolls?

9. Will any new Hanson merchandise be coming out soon?

10. True or false: Isaac, Taylor, and Zachary do not have girlfriends.

Answers to New and Upcoming

Don't be surprised if Hanson adds even more instruments to their repertoire in the coming years. When asked what the future holds, Ike said, "We have a lot more to strive for," and Zac added, "And lots more instruments to learn!"

1. Six. That means they'll make at least four more!

2. False. That was just a suggestion in *People* magazine that swelled into a rumor.

3. Yes. The brothers have been in negotiations to make a fun movie loosely based on their life, similar to the Beatles' *A Hard Day's Night*.

4. Galt Neiderhoffer.

5. *Hurricane Streets* writer Morgan J. Freeman.

6. The possibility of a weekly Hanson TV series.

7. Comedy. You can bet it would be a light-

hearted, fun show that would capture the group's energy. Sources close to the band have said the series would be like *The Monkees*.

8. No. The boys regard such marketing efforts as cheesy.

9. You bet! The group's management has been hard at work creating new Hanson posters, T-shirts, stickers, and other collectibles for 1998.

10. True, but not for lack of interest. However, 1997 was such a busy year that the brothers had no time for dating. Perhaps they'll find time in 1998. Now, that's something to look forward to!

9

MEASURING UP WITH OTHER FANS

The combined ages of Isaac, Taylor, and Zachary add up to about forty-four. That's still younger than many of your teachers! It's no wonder that, when it comes to Hanson, they just don't get it.

So now comes the defining moment. Your friends and classmates can argue that they have more pinups or know more Hanson songs by heart, but if you scored better on these quizzes, they can learn a lot about Hanson from you.

Scoring

Check your answers in each section and mark those that are correct. Then write the number of correct answers from each section on the corresponding space below. Last, add up these numbers to get your total and then compare the numbers with your friends' to see how well you did and how you measure up with other Hanson fans you know.

Band Basics (25)	_____
Zac's Pop Quiz (25)	_____
Taylor Test (25)	_____
Isaac Exam (25)	_____
Who Said That? (25)	_____
Discography (50)	_____
Appearance Is Everything (50)	_____
New and Upcoming (10)	_____
Total	_____

All 235 correct: Zac, what are you doing with this book? Shouldn't you be practicing your drums or something?

More than 200 correct: There's no doubt about it, you're in select company! Very few Hanson fans know this much about them. Are you sure you're not a distant cousin? Maybe you should get a job with the record company. Way to go!

150–199 correct: Nice job! You know enough about Hanson to qualify as a fanatic! Make sure you don't neglect your homework in the course of your quest for Hanson info, or your 'rents might get a bit peeved.

100–149 correct: You're definitely down with Hanson! You know quite a bit about Ike, Tay, and Zac, but not quite enough to brag that you're Hanson's number one fan.

50-99 correct: You might know a thing or two about Hanson, but let's face it, you've got some Hanson homework to do. Better spend more time checking out Websites and reading teen mags.

Fewer than 50 correct: You call yourself a Hanson fan? You probably know a few of their songs, but they're not your favorite group. Maybe the next album will get you hooked on Hanson!

10

WEBSITES AND OTHER INFO SOURCES

The Hanson boys have learned a great deal in the course of their travels. They've absorbed the culture and history of nearly one hundred cities in more than a dozen countries.

The best place to find up-to-date information on Hanson is the Internet. The official Hanson Website and the Mercury Records Hanson Website are brimming with the latest information. If that's not enough for you, there are seventy different fan-produced Hanson sites from all around the world. There are also eight sites devoted to Zac, seven to Taylor, and six to Isaac. You'll find ten chat rooms where you can gossip with other fanatics, and you could even log on to twenty-five anti-Hanson sites. (Believe it or not, not everybody loves Hanson.) If this doesn't satisfy your Hanson hunger, then you need to pack your bags and start following the band around the globe!

Following is a review of some of the best Hanson Websites as well as a few ways to get

Hanson information if you're not on-line. Remember that unofficial Websites come and go. Also, all it takes to create a Website is a little know-how and a few bucks, so what appears in these sites may not always be accurate. Keep in mind, too, that if you use "Hanson" as a key word, you'll call up some sites that have nothing to do with the band. One thing you'll see pop up often is a Florida area real estate company. After all, the brothers are not the only ones with that last name! To avoid this problem, narrow your subject search to music only.

It may sound "Weird," but the next time you ask yourself, "Where's The Love?" hop on-line and you'll find Hanson info and other Hanson fans in an "MMMBop"! These Websites should keep you plenty busy the next time you get "Snowed In."

THE OFFICIAL WEBSITES

The Hanson Site:
www.hansonline.com

The developers of this Website work closely with Hanson and their management to ensure that all of the information posted is accurate. Another great feature of this site is that it often includes personal messages from Ike, Tay, and Zac to their fans. Log on to the address above for links to Lyrics, Press, Fans, Hanson Chat, Merchandise, Bio, Live Updates, and Video/New Pics.

The Mercury Records Site:
www.mercuryrecords.com/mercury/artists/hanson

Hanson's record company is another great source of accurate information on the band. This site includes album information, breaking news, a link to the official site, and some terrific contests that give you the opportunity to win Hanson merchandise and autographed CDs and videos. There's also a link that allows you to check out other great Mercury Records artists like Radish and the Mighty Mighty Bosstones.

THE BEST UNOFFICIAL WEBSITES

Hanson HITZ:
www.hansonhitz.com

This is the only unofficial site that's endorsed by Hanson. You may, at some point, check out the official sites and find that they haven't been updated in a while. This happens sometimes, because the creators of those sites work with Hanson and are therefore just as busy. On those occasions, surf over to *Hanson HITZ* for informative, up-to-the-minute Hanson news. Links include Articles, FAQs, Lyrics, Pictures, Chat, and Clips.

If you're a Mac user, however, one downside to this site is that the screen comes up with a blue background and can sometimes be difficult to read.

Hanson Addicts Anonymous:
www.geocities.com/SunsetStrip/Stage/7698

Hanson Addicts Anonymous is one of the most popular Hanson Websites on the Internet, and with good reason. If you're looking for strange and hard-to-find tidbits, like what kind of shampoo Taylor uses and what kind of underwear Isaac wears, then this is the place for you.

My Little Tribute to Hanson:
users.aol.com/nadaace/hanson.html

This fast-growing site was developed by two guys in high school. Don't let that stop you from checking it out, though. Judging by the wealth of interesting facts they've posted, these guys are definitely in tune.

Gotta Have Hanson:
www.geocities.com/Sunset Strip/Palladium/7311/ghh

This should be the first place you look for facts on each individual Hanson brother. Through this Website you'll find links to *Gotta Have Isaac,* *Gotta Have Taylor,* and *Gotta Have Zac.* Each page includes little-known facts on each brother.

Zac Shack:
www.angelfire.com/az/ZacShack

For some adorable Zac photos, head for the Zac Shack. Log on to this address and you'll also find a cool contest and a rundown of some of Zac's most embarrassing moments!

Taylor Hanson Fan Page:
www.geocities.com/SunsetStrip/palladium/4142

If you're completely obsessed with Taylor, look no further. This Website features countless submissions from fans who are head over heels for Taylor. Fans from all over the world send their Taylor poems, rumors, encounter stories, and even dreams to this place. This site even has a scrawl wall and a chat room so that you can swap Tay stories with new on-line friends.

Hot Isaac Hanson Page:
www.geocities.com/SunsetStrip/Stage/3988

This Web page has a dynamite layout of photos and graphics. Check this one out if you're in search of new Ike pictures.

Ike Hanson:
members.tripod.com/~Hanson_luver

If you're on the lookout for information and quotes, this site is chock-full of what you need. You'll find a thorough list of Ike's most memorable quotes, and there are links to Zac and Tay quotes, too!

OTHER HANSON WEBSITES

Here is a list of all of the unofficial Websites that were available at the time this book was written.

Hanson

A.D.I.D.A.H. (All Day I Dream About Hanson)
Above 'n' Beyond
A.J.'s Hanson Page
Albertane's Hanson Page
All Day and Night Hanson
Anna's Hanson Place
Ashlee and Ashley's Hanson Homepage
Danish Hanson Page
Dutch Hanson Page
Ebeth's Hanson Page
ElectricAngel's Hanson Page
Eli's Hanson Site
Fly the Wings of an Eagle
Hanson Addicts Anonymous
*Hanson and Metallica: Thinking of You Nothing
    Else Matters*
Hanson Around the World
Hanson Australia

HANSON

Hanson Cafe
Hanson Central
Hanson Crazed
Hanson Crazy
Hanson Down Under
Hanson Fan Club Page
Hanson Fan Page
Hanson, Hanson, Hanson
Hanson Headquarters
Hanson Hotspot
Hanson Land
Hanson Luver's Place
Hanson Mania
Hanson Maniacs Anonymous
Hanson Opinion Page
Hanson Pages
Hanson Paradise
Hanson Place
Hanson Planet
Hanson Site
Hanson Source
Hanson 3D
HansonWeb.com
Here's . . . Hanson
Honestly Hanson
ITZ Central
Jennifer's Hanson Homepage
Lisa's Taylor Hanson Page
Loser-Free I Happen to Like Hanson Page
Marie's Hanson Mansion
Marilyn Hanson

Meghan's Hanson Page
Melanie's Hanson Page
Mmmbop All the Way
Mmmbop—Are You Still Here?
MMMBopin' Fest of Hanson
MMMHanson
Monika's Hanson Page
My Little Tribute to Hanson
Official Anti Anti-Hanson Page
One Fine Page for One Fine Group
Phenomenon: Hanson
Planet Hanson
Play the Hanson Game
Ryan's Hanson Page
SpanisHanson's Page
Twicm's Hanson Page
Vicky's Salute to Hanson
Wacky Hanson Page
Usenet—alt.fan.hanson

Zac

Ali's Zac Hanson Page
Becah's Zachary Hanson Web Page
Daize's Zac in the Box Page
Gwen's Zac Hanson Page
Zac Hanson Bus Stop
Zac Page
Zac Shack
Zoe's Zac Hanson Page

Taylor

Gwen's Taylor Hanson Page
Jordan Taylor Hanson
Taylor Hanson Fan Page
Taylor Hanson Page
Taylor Hanson Web Page
Taylor!
Taylor Taylor Taylor

Isaac

Clarke Isaac Hanson
Gwen's Ike Hanson Page
Hot Isaac Hanson Page
Ike Hanson
Isaac Hanson Appreciation Page
LoveHanson's Isaac Hanson Web Page

OTHER INFO SOURCES

Internet Sites

Links to other sites:
members.aol.com.Crescent14/hlink.html

Hanson fact sheet:
members.aol.com/GSquiggles/hansonfacts.html

Fan club E-mail:
hansonfans@hansonline.com

Addresses and Phone Numbers

Official Fan Club (Send a self-addressed stamped envelope to receive fan club information):
Hanson
c/o HITZ List
Box 703136
Tulsa, OK 74170

Record Company:
Hanson
c/o Mercury Records
11150 Santa Monica Blvd.
Suite 1100
Los Angeles, CA 90025
or
c/o Mercury Records
825 Eighth Avenue
New York, NY 10019

Management:
Hanson
c/o Triune Music Group
8322 Livingston Way
Los Angeles, CA 90046

Official Hanson Phone Hotline (long-distance charges apply):
(918) 446-3979

ABOUT THE AUTHOR

Matt Netter is a freelance writer who lives and works in New York City. He is also the author of *Zac Hanson: Totally Zac!*

Make sure you have the bestselling Hanson books with all the info on Taylor, Isaac, and Zac, each with eight pages of color photos!

MMMBop to the Top
By Jill Matthews

TOTALLY TAYLOR!
By Nancy Krulik

TOTALLY ZAC!
By Matt Netter

TOTALLY IKE!
By Nancy Krulik